A Manual of

A DEFINITIVE GUIDE TO SERIES

HASTINGS HOUSE PUBLISHERS NEW YORK 22

Script Typefaces

IN CURRENT USE, SELECTED AND

ARRANGED WITH AN INTRODUCTION

COMMENTARIES AND APPENDICES

BY R S HUTCHINGS

CORY ADAMS & MACKAY LTD LONDON

First published 1965 by Cory, Adams & Mackay Ltd
39 Sloane Street, London S.W.1
Printed and made in Great Britain
by W. & J. Mackay & Co Ltd, Chatham

Introduction

TYPOGRAPHERS know what they mean when they speak of scripts, but most of them would find it difficult to define the term precisely to anyone unfamiliar with the broad field of type design. To the typographical historian 'A script type is one cut in imitation of current handwriting, not of the cursive book hands, but of the ordinary script in everyday use'.[1] The principle is clear, but to be applicable to the entire range of such faces available today a somewhat wider definition would be needed. Some formal scripts derive from hands that are as remote from present-day currency as the ancestors of roman and italic book faces, and some contemporary informal scripts imitate eccentric kinds of handwriting that could hardly be claimed to be 'current' today.

There is a clear-cut distinction between the designs we call scripts, and cursive faces such as italic and fraktur that derive more directly from handwriting than standard roman types; and, as an additional distinction, italics are now designed to accompany equivalent romans. This is generally understood, but it should be added that some undoubted scripts are just as formalized in the component elements of their characters as regular italics.

At the other end of the scale, many contemporary display types are unhesitatingly classified as scripts because of their evident calligraphic or brush-drawn origins, although they may be neither 'in imitation of current handwriting' nor 'ordinary' scripts 'in everyday use'. There are many such faces today, differing very widely in their forms, and it is difficult to draw a precise boundary beyond which the illusion of spontaneity becomes sufficiently disciplined to transform a script into a display italic with merely incidental allusion to written or drawn origins. The question is further confused by the fact that many 'self-evident' scripts are upright, and some of them employ roman,

[1] A. F. Johnson: *Type Designs* (2nd edn; Grafton, 1959).

not italic, lower-case forms. It should also be added that the nature of the designer's tool is not in itself relevant, since with present-day methods of pantographic punch and matrix manufacture any kind of typeface can leave the design stage in the form of pen or brush drawings.

In the absence of a fully comprehensive definition, the term 'script' must be confined to those faces that are commonly assigned to this category within the working typographical field. This is perhaps an unsatisfactory position in principle—and one to which the national standards institutions may apply themselves in due course—but in practice it leaves surprisingly little scope for uncertainties or controversy. For the purpose of this survey, therefore, and of the check list accompanying it, script types are assumed to be either (1) formal or semi-formal cursives outside the book-face traditions of italic, gothic texts, uncials, etc; or (2) informal and ostensibly spontaneously written or drawn faces that have not been regularized within traditional typographical conventions. Thus, in the first category, *Mayfair Cursive* (Ludlow) is included, although many of its lower-case characters are of orthodox italic form; and in the second category, *Klang* (Monotype) and *Lydian Roman* and *Italic* (ATF)—despite their drawn derivation—are excluded, although *Lydian Cursive* is included.

The early history of script types, and of the current hands from which they derived, and of their separation from the 'mainstream' italic tradition, is of considerable interest in itself, but has very slight bearing on the study of present-day script designs. In general terms, all scripts used for the Western European languages—that is to say, excluding cyrillics, Greeks, and other 'exotics'—stem from either gothic or latin written forms, with the minor exception of uncials which, in fact, have no current representatives that are generally accepted as script faces. The gothic line comprises the civilité types of the sixteenth and seventeenth centuries, a few of which survive in matrix form but are no longer cast; a few faces of more recent production that derive from them more or less remotely; and some German black-letter cursives of which only one is still current. All other script types in general use today within the languages based on the roman and italic alphabets are of latin descent, although it should be added that some contemporary informal designs show traces of gothic influence that may sometimes be unconscious and are unlikely to be evident to the average user or reader.

With the exception of traditional copperplate formal scripts there are virtually no script designs in general use today that were available before 1925, and the majority have been produced since 1945. Until well into the 1930s it was exceptional for even a well-stocked composing room to hold more than a single script series, and their use was restricted almost exclusively to the circumscribed field of professional and social stationery: visiting cards, letterheads, invitations, funeral notices, etc. A very few alternatives to formal copperplate designs were available in the upright French ronde tradition, but their use was equally limited and they were largely overshadowed by the more familiar inclined scripts in the nineteenth-century copybook tradition.

Fel

PARISIAN RONDE

There were also a few display scripts of heavier weight and greater freedom of design, although they would be regarded as relatively formal in conception in comparison with most of the popular postwar faces. The typefounders had made intermittent attempts to popularize display scripts since about 1890, but with little sense of direction or continuity, and with little encouragement from the printers and their customers. Scripts of this period were more or less based on current cursive signwriting styles, and although most of them owed something to the prevailing 'civil service' round-hand that superseded the Victorian copperplate writing, they made little attempt to simulate any convincing degree of hand-written or hand-drawn character. The last typical representative series of this kind to be issued was probably Stephenson Blake's *Glenmoy* (1931), which, like most similar series from other foundries, has been withdrawn since the last war. One typical example that is still available—and is illustrated in this volume—is Monotype *Script Heavy* 322, which was originally issued by Ludwig & Mayer in Germany in 1926.

Prin

GLENMOY

These early display scripts were in essence the degenerate descendants of the early- and mid-nineteenth-century fat-faces and bold sans and egyptians. The evident conclusion is that the Victorian punchcutters turned to script display forms too late to apply their skill and creative ability to them with any zest: by the 1890s their initiative had been sapped from two directions— from the litho artists, who could create novelties for every individual job, and from the 'pirate' typefounders who could make electrotype matrices of every new type series as soon as it appeared. In fact, the full potentialities of script design awaited pantographic methods of engraving for their exploitation, and although these methods were available from the 1880s it was not until after the First World War that effective advantage was taken of their ability to reproduce designs conceived and completed on the drawing board.

The great majority of script types available and in regular use today therefore have little historical background, and many of them can claim no derivation or direct precedent within the typographic tradition. In this connexion it is very much to the credit of typefounders and composing-machine manufacturers that they have retained a large measure of initiative and that new designs originating as type often enjoy considerable influence in other media.

To the new-comer to the typographic world, faced with a bewildering choice of scripts ranging from the politely formal to the outrageously heterodox, it must be difficult to realize that both their profusion and their fashionable status are comparatively recent phenomena. Such script faces as were available after the First World War were ignored by the pioneers and later adherents of what has become known as 'the typographical renaissance' of the 1920s, which significantly transformed the face of the graphic arts—not only in Britain but much wider afield—during the following two or three decades.

The use of copperplate scripts in sophisticated display functions, and especially in Press advertising, was still a daring innovation with a slightly suspect Germanic flavour as late as 1935. The trend gained some ground, however, in the following prewar years, perhaps encouraged by the introduction of several series of heavier weight than had hitherto been available—such as *Marina* from Stephenson Blake, and the even bolder *Commercial* and *Bank Scripts* from ATF, which were originally produced earlier in the century, but had not previously been imported to Britain. Meanwhile, several contemporary formal scripts outside the copperplate tradition—such as *Bernhard Cursive* (Bauer, 1925, also issued by Stephenson Blake the following year as *Madonna Ronde*) and *Trafton Script* (Bauer, 1933)—began to be widely used within the British printing industry, and also in the United States, although they made comparatively little impact on Press advertising.

The first distinctively contemporary display script to gain widespread acceptance was *Holla*, designed by Rudolf Koch for

Five

BANK SCRIPT

The

HOLLA

8

Klingspor in 1932. This series might well be claimed as the direct forerunner of most of the characteristic informal display scripts of today, and opened up a new field of design based on highly personal treatments of pen and brush techniques. The trend still continues vigorously, and a large proportion of the new display scripts of recent years have clearly been influenced by Koch's innovation.

Parallel with the increasing popularity of informal designs deriving from pen and brush since the end of the last war, a fresh lease of life has been gained by the traditional copperplate school of scripts as a result of the introduction of a number of new designs better suited to display functions than their predecessors. There are also signs—of which more will be said later in this introduction—of new approaches by type designers to the problems of equating convention and originality in this highly formalized and long-static typeface category.

Since about the year 1930, therefore, a revolution has occurred in the production and use of script types. From being the most neglected and limited group of designs they have become one of the most varied and eclectic; they have attracted the attentions of enterprising and able designers—some of them from beyond the boundaries of the typographic field—and they now enjoy a 'fashion status' among typographers and art directors that is without historical precedent. In order to understand this phenomenon more clearly it may be useful to look at the main categories of modern script design in greater detail.

Formal copperplate scripts in the nineteenth-century copybook tradition derive from the models of the eighteenth-century writing masters. The 'Italian hand', as it was called, was intrinsically an engraved form, although it was well adapted to personal use after the introduction of steel pens, which provided a greater control over stroke formation and variations of shading than sharpened quills. The last English script of gothic derivation is said to have been cut about 1765 by Thomas Cottrell, and in 1774 the same founder produced a latin script which was destined to have far-reaching influence at home and abroad and can be regarded as the direct origin of the formal copperplate style. He increased the angle of slope, eliminated the serifs and other conventional elements that had gradually invaded the preceding *rondes* and scriptorials, and fitted his characters so closely together as to give the impression of actual continuity.

9

His innovation was immediately followed by his competitors and in particular by the French founders, who gave script of this kind the generic name '*anglaise*', by which it has been known on the Continent ever since. By the early years of the nineteenth century the new style was firmly established. A great deal of ingenuity in engraving, casting and finishing had been devoted to connecting adjacent letters by means of hairlines that made direct contact when set, and angle-body moulds were subsequently introduced as a means of simplifying this problem.

The conventions of the *anglaise* style were rigidly maintained by succeeding generations, and many series still cast are virtually identical to those of Firmin Didot issued in 1809. Towards the end of the century there was a tendency for capitals to acquire more flourishes, and the German foundries produced a number of highly condensed series, but in other respects the tradition remained rigidly crystallized until the introduction of bolder weights for display functions within the present century. The first of these was *Bank Script*, issued by the Chicago foundry of Barnhart Brothers & Spindler (later absorbed by ATF) in 1911, followed by ATF's *Commercial Script* in 1925. Neither of these series—which appear to have had no contemporary counterparts in Europe—appear to have been used to any significant extent outside the traditional functions of copperplate until the 1930s, when both of them were discovered by British advertising typographers. Comparable series are now cast by European founders, notably Bauer's *Cantate*, issued in 1958.

There have also been a number of new series in recent years of light and medium weight, some of which return to the simplest forms of the earliest designs, and others that introduce new features within the limits of the accepted conventions. Thus, *Juliet* (Nebiolo, 1955) goes back to the light weight and open curves of the early models, while *Youthline* (Stephenson Blake, 1952) ingeniously avoids direct contacts while suggesting continuity; and both *Diane* (Olive, 1956) and *Amazone* (Amsterdam, 1959) elaborate the copperplate theme without actually losing contact with the established tradition.

There is no parallel to this instance of a group of type designs that remained immobile, both in design and in limits of function, for upwards of 150 years, and then embarking on a new period of development and new applications in the wider sphere of typographical display. This is not just another instance of revival, since scripts of this class were never abandoned; and not simply

COMMERCIAL
SCRIPT

CANTATE

DIANE

a matter of a return to popularity, since it is unlikely that they were ever used any more widely than during the years immediately prior to their elevation to fashionable status.

The fact is that a long-neglected style of type design that until recently was regarded as inherently sterile and incapable of further growth has gradually but persistently acquired a new significance to designers of printing. The trend has been too gradual and too persistent in its course to be dismissed as a casual and arbitrary whim of fashion. It has been accentuated, perhaps, by the prevailing nostalgia for Victorian styles, and it may have been delayed at the start by the fact that copperplate was still, until at least the 1920s, the theoretical basis of colloquial handwriting.

In addition to the copperplate scripts of the *anglaise* tradition there is a clearly defined category of formal scripts of less standardized design. Such scripts are essentially engraved, rather than pen-written or brush-drawn letters, and although they are found in a variety of forms, most of them derive—in principle if not always in detail—from the French *rondes* of the late eighteenth and early nineteenth century, which in turn descended from the 'scriptorials' used for the engrossing of legal documents after the abandonment of gothic scripts in the previous century.

Monotype *Dorchester Script*, issued in 1938, is closely related to the scriptorials shown by the Grover Foundry towards the end of the seventeenth century and used for some of the early news-sheets. Stephenson Blake's *Parisian Ronde* is characteristic of the French nineteenth-century style—upright, with joining lower-case, looped ascenders, hooked descenders, and flourished but compact capitals.

Hock

Although these series (and other similar designs no longer available) have long been used in the same limited field of social stationery as the *anglaise* scripts, they have not shared their rise to wider currency, and are probably unlikely to do so within the foreseeable future. There remains, however, some scope for comparable but not directly related designs that share many of the characteristics of the *rondes* and their predecessors.

There has been a slender but continuous succession of such faces since the early 1930s, commencing with *Bernhard Cursive* and *Trafton Script*—to which reference was made earlier in this introduction—and continuing with such examples as *Ariston Script* (Berthold, 1933) and Weber's *Forelle*, introduced into

11

Britain in 1938 as *Mercury*; and, since the war, *Stradivarius* (Bauer, 1946), *Fluidum* (Nebiolo, 1951), and *Boulevard* (Berthold, 1955).

The extent to which designs of this kind have achieved some measure of popularity is probably unrelated to that of the orthodox copperplate scripts, and has probably been retarded, rather than assisted, by the parallel but incidental rise to fashionable demand of the informal pen and brush scripts. Both *Bernhard Cursive* (also cast by Stephenson Blake since 1926) and *Trafton Script* were widely used during the years prior to the arrival of the many bolder and more vigorous informal scripts now available, and which are generally preferred by publicity typographers. The formal designs—including the more recently issued examples—have remained in demand, but it is significant that the demand is from printers rather than from the art directors and advertising men, whose preferences largely determine the sales of the informal pen and brush scripts. One limiting factor in the production and marketing of new non-traditional formal scripts is that they tend to become outdated more rapidly than either standard copperplate designs on the one hand or informal designs on the other. This is a problem that still challenges the ingenuity of type designers, and there remains promising scope for the creation of contemporary formal scripts sufficiently novel to appeal to the publicity world and yet sufficiently free from eccentricity to enjoy longer-term popularity among printers.

Typefaces based on freely-drawn pen and brush techniques are a comparatively recent phenomenon, and some reasons for this apparent oversight of typographical history have been suggested in the earlier part of this introduction. It is surely surprising, on closer reflection, that their possibilities were either undiscovered or ignored by the nineteenth-century typefounders and their punchcutters during the adventurous decades before the challenges of the litho artists and the electrotyping pirates took full effect. One might imagine, from studying the specimen books of the 1940s and 1950s, for instance, that brush-drawn scripts—complete with ragged edges and perhaps loose spots of superfluous paint to be added by the compositor according to fancy—would have made a particularly strong appeal to the designers of ornate tuscans with trellised backgrounds and fatfaces interlaced with flowering foliage. Perhaps they regarded 'action' type designing that—in principle, at least—is within every literate's reach as an unworthy challenge to their hard-won skills; or possibly—as Mrs Gray has suggested in connexion with the paucity of rustic types—'the Victorians were not altogether bereft of a sense of their material'.[1]

The manual dexterity required to simulate authentic pen and brush strokes would certainly not have been beyond the virtuosity of the hand punchcutters of the Victorian age, and, as it happens, the first really significant informal display script in the modern sense was engraved by hand by its own designer. This was Rudolf Koch's *Holla*, the earliest notably successful attempt to exploit convincingly hand-drawn qualities in the design of a script that staked its claim as a general-purpose display face rather than as reproduction calligraphy.

The typical informal display scripts of the present century, however—and the overwhelming majority of them—have been pantographically produced, and indeed are among the most impressive achievements of mechanical engraving. It is another paradox of typographical history that it was almost fifty years after the invention of the punchcutting pantograph that its intrinsic suitability for the reproduction of pen and brush letters with authentic qualities of informality began to be appreciated and exploited.

Informal scripts cannot readily be classified, and resist precise definitions even more strongly than the script category of type design as a whole. It is superficially tempting, when studying this field, to attempt an exact division between pen-written and brush-drawn styles, but in practice the distinction is difficult to maintain. Apart from the more orthodox designs that exploit the 'natural' usage of pen and brush there are many instances of 'hybrid' approaches employing lettering tools of various breadths and cuts, and of brushwork adopted to calligraphic styles.

The greater number of the more characteristic contemporary informal scripts derive—at least nominally—from brush treatments, but there is still a hankering after genuinely informal calligraphic faces retaining both the weight and the stroke formation of true handwriting that, however individual in its idiosyncrasies, employs a conventional writing tool rather than a studio lettering tool or brush. There can be no doubt, however, that type designers will continue to experiment with

The

PEPITA

Bat

MISTRAL

[1] Nicolette Gray: *Nineteenth Century Ornamented Types & Title Pages* (Faber, 1938).

15

unconventional tools and treatments, and that even the most free-and-easy 'slap-dash' effects must eventually come to terms with the drawing board.

The extent to which the postwar spate of new script types can be expected to continue will not depend primarily on the creative ability of type designers but on the economics of type production and marketing. It is a question fraught with paradoxes, and sooner or later most of the answers will almost certainly be found outside the traditional boundaries of typefounding. New display faces—particularly informal scripts—need to be original in order to be produced profitably, and the more original they are the shorter do their prospects of profitable life tend to be. A related factor is that in these days of national and international advertising campaigns for mass-produced consumer products it is possible for a new display face to appear to be successful overnight, although its apparent success may represent very meagre sales, and may also discourage other potential buyers.

It seems reasonable to assume that the long-term prospects for display types in the script field will lie in filmsetting rather than in traditional typefounding and hot-metal composing machines. Already there are signs of a tendency for new script types to derive from film rather than for filmsetting methods to reproduce scripts already available in metal. The *Dom* family, for example, was originally popularized by the American trade service operated by Photolettering Inc. before being cut in type by the American Type Founders Corporation, and several of the filmsetting systems are building up ranges of script faces not available in cast type. It should also be noted that filmsetting techniques offer fruitful scope for the exploitation of script type designs with unprecedented freedom from physical limitations. The ultimate outcome will almost certainly involve closer association of the more enterprising of the world's typefoundries with filmsetting interests, so that their creative and technical facilities and knowledge of market requirements can be put to service in new fields.

Pack

DOM CASUAL

Alphabets and Commentaries

ABCDEFGHIJK

LMNOPQRST

UVWXY&Z

abcdefghijklmnopqrstuvwxyz

1234567890

The first script types—as distinct from the early italic book faces—derived from gothic manuscript hands, and date from the middle of the sixteenth century. Some original matrices of this period survive, but no historically authentic types are publicly available today. The representative example shown here was designed by Morris F. Benton in 1922 and was based—with considerable modification—on a *civilité* believed to have been cut by Robert Granjon in 1557.

ABCDEFGHIJKLMNOPQRSTUV

WXY&Z

abcdefghijklmnopqrstuvwxyz

22 pt UNION PEARL (STEPHENSON BLAKE)

ABCDEFGHIJKLMNO

PQRSTUVWXY&Z

abcdefghijklmnopqrstuvwxyz

1234567890

36 pt DORCHESTER SCRIPT 436 (MONOTYPE)

Latin script types, known as 'cursorials' and deriving from current handwriting, came into use towards the end of the seventeenth century and were used to set some of the earliest news-sheets. Union Pearl, of which the original matrices survive, was one of a range of scripts shown by the Grover Foundry in London during this period. Dorchester Script, issued in 1938, resembles another of the Grover scripts, used in Ichabod Dawkes's *News Letter* from 1698.

18

$ABCDEFGHIJK$
$LMNOPQRSTU$
$VWXY$ & Z

abcdefghijklmnopqrstuvwxyz

1234567890

48 pt PARISIAN RONDE (STEPHENSON BLAKE)

$ABCDEFGHIJKLMN$
$OPQRSTUVWXY$ & Z

abcdefghijklmnopqrstuvwxyz

1234567890

24 pt IMPERIAL SCRIPT (STEPHENSON BLAKE)

Formal upright scripts known as 'rondes'—latinized derivations from *civilité*—were widely used in France and elsewhere during the eighteenth and nineteenth centuries. This comparatively modern example was acquired by its present founders from the Inland Type Foundry (USA) in 1905, but probably originated in France.

Meanwhile, sloped scripts in the copperplate tradition of the 'Italian hand' writing books were introduced in England by Cottrell about 1774, and were developed in France, where they became known as *anglaise*. Imperial Script is a late-nineteenth-century example that closely resembles Firmin Didot's *Anglaise* issued in Paris in 1809.

19

A B C D E F

G H I J K L M N O P

Q R S T U V W

X Y & Z

abcdefghijklmnopqrstuv

œ   *wxyz*   *œ*

1234567890

42 pt PALACE SCRIPT (STEPHENSON BLAKE)

Formal copperplate scripts became rigidly conventionalized early in the nineteenth century, and innumerable series were produced—and many are still available—differing only in minute details. This example, engraved by the founders in 1923, is representative of the lighter weight long used in the composition of business and social stationery.

ABCDEFGH

IJKLMNOPQ

RSTUVW

XY&Z

abcdefghijklmnopqrstuv

æ   wxyz   œ

1234567890

48 pt MARINA SCRIPT (STEPHENSON BLAKE)

During the years between the world wars copperplate scripts began gradually to be
used in general display functions, and somewhat heavier weights were called for.
This example, which is one of the most widely used of its kind,
was engraved by Stephenson Blake in 1936.

A B C D E F G

H I J K L M

N O P Q R S

T U V W X

Y & Z Th W K

I J N E V W

Æ Œ

abcdefghijklmnopqrstuvw

xyz e rsftzœœ IVX

1234567890

48 D IDEAL SCHREIBSCHRIFT 3 (STEMPEL)

In Germany and elsewhere on the Continent during the same period a demand arose for copperplate scripts more condensed in set than had previously been available. This example was designed by Franz Riedinger for the former Krebs Foundry in 1927, and subsequently passed to the present founders.

ABCDEFGHIJKL

MNOPQRST

UVWXYZ

abcdefghijklmnopqrs

tuvwxyz

1234567890

48 pt COMMERCIAL SCRIPT (ATF)

Bold copperplate scripts originated in America: the first was Bank Script, issued by
the former Barnhart Bros & Spindler Foundry of Chicago in 1911, followed by
Commercial Script in 1925. Both series are now cast by ATF.

24

A B C D E F G

H I J K L M N O

P Q R S T U V

W X Y & Z

a b c d e f g h i j k l m n o p q

r s t u v w x y z

1 2 3 4 5 6 7 8 9 0

48 pt YOUTHLINE SCRIPT (STEPHENSON BLAKE)

Since early in the nineteenth century copperplate scripts have been designed, engraved, cast and finished to provide continuous links between adjacent characters, necessitating special moulds and many kerns. This example, issued in 1952, avoids kerning and has been designed to give an impression of continuity without actual contacts.

60 pt JULIET (NEBIOLO)

This example, designed by Aldo Novarese in 1955, reverts to the characteristic nineteenth-century copperplate weight, but has a slight reduction of angle of inclination in order to permit casting on a square body.

ABCDEFGH
IJKLMNO
PQRSTUV
WXY&ZTh
ÆŒ

abcdefghijklmnopq
æ rstuvwxyz œ
1234567890

This is the boldest of the currently available scripts in the formal copperplate tradition, and was designed by J. J. Siercke in 1958.

ABCDEFGHI

JKLMNOPQR

STUVWXY&Z

abcdefghijklmnopqrstu

ck uuvxyzz ch

1234567890

48 D AMAZONE (AMSTERDAM)

Despite the rigid conventions of copperplate script design, there is still scope for ingenuity in the consistent application of minor modifications. This example, designed by L. H. D. Smits in 1959, exploits angular shading of the looped lower-case strokes.

ABCDEFGH
IJKLMNOP
QRSTUVW
XYZ

abcdefghijklmnopqrs

ae   tuvwxyz   oe

1234567890

36 D DIANE (OLIVE)

The long-static copperplate script tradition has indeed begun to challenge display
type designers in recent years. This example, designed by Roger Excoffon in 1956,
adopts abrupt shading and sheared stroke terminals, and is provided
with an alternative capital alphabet with additional flourishes.

A B C D E F G H I J K L M N

O P Q R S T U V W X Y & Z

abcdefghijklmnopqrstuvwxyz

ffifflffiffl   aemt   gg gy:~

1234567890

36 pt ARTSCRIPT (LANSTON MONOTYPE)

The *anglaise* tradition was not the sole source of formal script designs in modern times. The example shown here—designed by Sol Hess in 1940—was based on revived Spanish *cancelleresca* hands of the late eighteenth century.

ABCDEFGHIJ
KLMNOPQRS
TUVWXY&Z

abcdefghijklmnopqrstuvwxyz

1234567890

48 pt MAYFAIR CURSIVE (LUDLOW)

Other formal scripts of the present century approach closely to conventional italic forms and depend on swash capitals and subsidiary hair-strokes to some lower-case characters for their cursive characteristics. This example was designed by R. Hunter Middleton in 1932.

ABCDEFG
HIJKLMNO
PQRSTUV
WXY&Z

abcdefghijklmnopqrs

æ tuvwxyz oe

1234567890

60 pt TRAFTON SCRIPT (BAUER)

This series—designed by the American Howard A. Trafton for a German foundry in 1933—was the first notably successful formal script of the present century to depart entirely from historical precedents. It is too regularized to imply pen-stroke formation, but enjoys a freedom of outline without direct derivation.

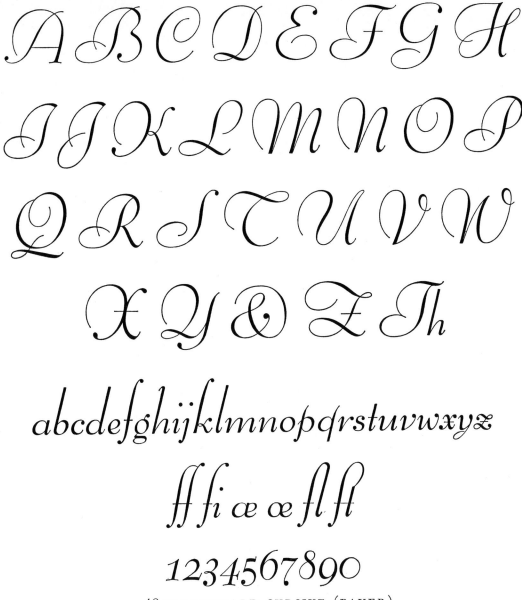

ABCDEFGH
IJKLMNOP
QRSTUVW
XY&ZTh

abcdefghijklmnopqrstuvwxyz

ſſ ſi œ œ fl ſt

1234567890

48 pt BERNHARD CURSIVE (BAUER)

This contemporary formal script and its bold variant were also designed by an American—Lucian Bernhard—and issued in Germany in 1925. They are also without direct historical precedent, but derive more from the *rondes* than from the *anglaise* school. Bernhard Cursive has also been cast by Stephenson Blake since 1926 as Madonna Ronde, to which was added in 1928 a bold variant (Madonna Bold) which is somewhat stouter in its lighter strokes than the Bauer series shown above.

33

A B C D E F G H

I J K L M N O P

Q R S T U V W

X Y & Z Th

abcdefghijklmnopqrs

ff fi œ tuvwxyz œ fl ft

1234567890

48 pt BERNHARD CURSIVE BOLD (BAUER)

34

ABCDEFGHI
JKLMNOPQRS
TUVWXY&Z

abcdefghijklmnopqrstu

vwxyz d e n r ſ

1234567890

48 pt GRACIA (AMSTERDAM)

This type from the Amsterdam Foundry is in a similar style but has more elegance.
It is based on Butterfly Light designed by Willy Schumann and issued
by Schriftguss in 1927.

35

ABCDEFGHIJ

KLMNOP

QRSTUVW

XYZ ÆŒ

abcdefghijklmnopqrstuv

wxyz fiflœœ

1234567890

ABCDEFGHI
JKLMNOP
QRSTUVW
XY&Z ÆŒ

abcdefghijklmnop
qrstuvwxyz fiflæœ

1234567890

48 D FORELLE AUSZEICHNUNG (WEBER)

These more freely conceived, but still formalized, series were designed by Erich Mallowitz and issued by Weber and other founders in 1936, and are also cast by Stephenson Blake as Mercury Light and Mercury respectively, although the former was re-engraved in Britain.

A B C D E F F. G

H I J K L M N O

P Q R S T U V

W X Y & Z

abcdefghijklmno

pqrstuvwxyz

1234567890

ABCDEFF.G
HIJKLMNO
PQRSTUVW
XY&Z
abcdefghijklmnop
qrstuvwxyz
1234567890

These series owe somewhat more to the *anglaise* tradition than most of the modern formal and semi-formal designs, and return to the convention of continuity between characters. They were designed by Martin Wilke in 1933 and 1934 respectively, and were originally accompanied by a bolder variant that has not been cast since the war.

48 pt STRADIVARIUS (BAUER)

This series, designed by Imre Reiner in 1945 and issued soon after the end of the
war, combines freely drawn but highly conventionalized capitals with a
compressed and somewhat squared-up lower-case alphabet.

40

36 pt BOULEVARD (BERTHOLD)

This series retains some links with the *anglaise* tradition, but its freedom of movement brings it to the limits of the formal division of script design.
It was designed by G. G. Lange in 1955.

ABCDEFGHIJK
LMNOPQRST
UVWXYZ
abcdefghijklmnopqr
stuvwxyz
1234567890

48 pt SCRIPT BOLD 332 (MONOTYPE)

The scripts illustrated on the previous pages were essentially *engraved* designs, with no direct relevance to colloquial handwriting of the present day. The example shown on this page, however, derives from a 'popular' hand of only yesterday, although its treatment makes no attempt to simulate pen- or brush-drawn strokes. This series was originally designed by E. Lautenbach and issued by Ludwig & Mayer in 1928 as *Prägefest*, although it was also exported from Germany as Samson Script.

ABCDEFGHIJKLMNOP

2RSTUVWXY&3

abcdefghijklmnopqrstuvw

xyz 1234567890

48 pt KAUFMANN SCRIPT (ATF)

ABCDEFGHIJKLMNO

P2RSTUVWXY&3

abcdefghijklmnopqrstuvw

xyz 1234567890

48 pt KAUFMANN BOLD (ATF)

Light-weight monotone scripts based on colloquial hands were produced towards the end of the nineteenth century and were used to set circulars—the equivalent function to that of modern typewriter faces. None of the earlier versions has survived, but the two more recent examples shown here—designed by M. R. Kaufmann in 1936—have retained their popularity. The bolder weight is also available on Monotype matrices as Swing Bold 585.

43

ABCDEFGHIJKL

MNOPQRSTUV

WXY&ZTh

abcdefghijklmnopqrst

œ uvwxyz œ

1234567890

ABCDEFGHIJKL

MNOPQRSTUV

WXY&ZTh

abcdefghijklmnopqrst

uvwxyz

1234567890

48 pt GILLIES GOTHIC BOLD (BAUER)

Monotone scripts were also produced during the 1930s with a view to their use in conjunction with the new twentieth-century sans designs. These two series were designed by W. S. Gillies in 1935, and were widely used at that time with the same foundry's Futura family.

ABCDEFGHIJ
KLMNOPQRS
TUVWXY&Z
abcdefghijklmnopq
rstuvwxyz1234567890

48 pt MANDATE (LUDLOW)

Display scripts based on conventionalized treatments of current handwriting were intermittently available from the 1880s, but very few were issued after 1920, and even fewer survived the arrival of the first informal contemporary scripts in the 1930s. The example shown above was designed as late as 1934 by R. Hunter Middleton, and continues in demand.

ABCDEFGHIJKLMNO
PQRSTUVWXYZ&Z

abcdefghijklmnopqrstuv
wxyz 1234567890

48 pt RHAPSODY (LUDWIG & MAYER)

Scripts based on 'sophisticated' rather than 'colloquial' hands usually exhibit a far closer simulation of pen-formed strokes than the formal and conventionalized examples previously shown. The series on this page, designed by Ilse Shuele in 1949, is inspired by the *schwabacher* hand. It may be considered as a long-range descendant of the early *civilité* types, and also provides an appropriate introduction to the current faces of calligraphic origins shown on the following pages.

A B C D E F G H I J

K L M N O P Q R S

J U V W X Y & Z

abcdefghijklmnopqrstuvwxyz &

1234567890

A F H J K L M V W

48 pt THOMPSON QUILLSCRIPT (ATF)

This series, designed by Tommy Thompson in 1953, is a colloquial version of the current revived form of chancery italic handwriting, and includes a number of alternative capitals. It is interesting to compare its characters and stroke formations in detail with italic book faces in the chancery tradition, such as Monotype Blado.

48

ABCDEFGHIJKLMN

OPQRSTUVWXY&Z

abcdefghijklmnopq

rstuvwxyz e

1234567890

48 pt LYDIAN CURSIVE (ATF)

This script variant of a family of type series based on broad penstroke techniques was designed by Warren Chappell in 1940. The cursive reveals some chancery influences, but its weight is intended for display functions.

ABCDEFGHIJ
KLMNOPQR
STUVWXY&Z
ÆŒ

abcdefghijklmnopqrstuv

wxyz 1234567890 aeœ

48 pt SCRIBE (DEBERNY & PEIGNOT)

Designed by Marcel Jacno in 1937, this is a broad-pen freehand design typical of
several series of its period, but with a marked individuality. It maintains joins
between most lower-case character combinations, but
not between capitals and lower-case.

ABCDEFGHI
JKLMNOPQ
RSTUVW
XY&Z

abcdefghijklmnopqrstuv

wxyz

1234567890

48 pt DERBY (BERTHOLD)

This forceful but sensitive broad-pen script shows some remote gothic derivation.
It was designed by G. G. Lange in 1953.

ABCDEFGHIJK
LMNOPQRST
UVWXY&Z

abcdefghijklmnopqrstu

vwxyz 1234567890 chckß

48 pt BRAVO (HAAS)

Another freely drawn broad-pen script, with traces—perhaps unconscious—of *civilité* influence. It was designed by E. A. Neukomm in 1945.

ABCDEFGH
IJKLMNOP
QRSTUVW
XY&Z

abcdefghijklmnopqrstuvwxyz

1234567890

48 pt ADMIRAL SCRIPT (LUDLOW)

This highly individual pen script is without direct historical derivation, but shows a very consistent formation of characters within its overall freedom of conception. It was designed by R. Hunter Middleton in 1960, and may be usefully contrasted with the same designer's Mandate Script, on page 46.

ABCDEFGHI

JKLMNOPQ

RSTUVWX

Y&ZTh

abcdefghijklmnopqrs

tuvwxyz th

1234567890

60 pt LEGEND (BAUER)

This very contemporary and highly personal pen script shows distinct signs of sixteenth-century gothic hand influences. It was designed by Professor Ernst Schneidler in 1937; it was the first series of its kind to be issued, and the first contemporary display script to employ non-standard logotype combinations to enhance the illusion of natural penmanship.

ABCDEFGHI
IJJKLMNOP
QuQ.RSTUV
WXYY&Z

abcdefghijklmnopqrstu
vwxyze n o r t

1234567890

48 pt RONDO (AMSTERDAM)

55

ABCDEFG
HIJKLMN
OPQRSTU
VWXY&Z

abcdefghijklmnopqrst

uvwxyz

Qu £1234567890

48 pt RONDO BOLD (AMSTERDAM)

This contemporary round-hand style owes something to the French *rondes* of the nineteenth century rather than to the English popular hand that was a degenerate descendant of formal copperplate. These two series were designed by Stefan Schlesinger and Dick Dooijes in 1948.

ABCDEFGHI
JKLMNOPQ
RSTUVW
XY&Z
abcdefghijklmn
opqrstuvwxyz
1234567890

48 pt MERCURIUS BOLD SCRIPT 584 (MONOTYPE)

The angular shadings to lower-case characters and the egyptian-like serifs of the capitals result from the use of a bamboo writing instrument in the design of this series by Imre Reiner, in 1957.

ABCDEFGH
IJKLMNOP
QRSTUVWX
ÆŒ Y&Z GTQu

abcdefghijklmnopqrstuv

ffffiflft   wxyz   sllttz

æœ 1234567890 IVX

ABCDEF GH

IJKLMNO

PQRSTUVWX

ÆŒ Y&Z GTQu

abcdefghijklmnopqrst

ffffiflft uvwxyz slltttz

æœ 1234567890 IVX

48 pt DISKUS SEMI-BOLD (STEMPEL)

Although these series retain pen-formed strokes and are free in their overall conception, they are as firmly disciplined as the non-traditional formal scripts of the Trafton era. They were designed by Martin Wilke in 1955 and 1956 respectively.

59

ABCDEFGHIJ
KLMNOPQRS
TUVWXY&Z

abcdefghijklmnopqrstuvwxyz

tt th t e s

£1234567890

72 pt REINER SCRIPT (AMSTERDAM)

A vigorous, almost upright script apparently formed by means of a broad but very resilient writing instrument. There are abrupt shadings and vestigial serifs, the capitals are outsized in relation to the lower-case, and most of them descend below the lower-case line. It was designed by Imre Reiner in 1951.

60

ABCDEFGH
IJKLMNO
PQRSTUV
WXY&Z

abcdefghijklmnopq

rstuvwxyz

1234567890

48 pt FLAIR (LUDLOW)

Evidently formed with a broad steel lettering-pen held at varying angles, this original script features eccentric contrasts of stroke weight between capitals and lower-case, with some alternative broad-stroke lower-case ascenders and descenders. It was designed by R. Hunter Middleton in 1961.

ABCDEFGHIJKL MNOPQRSTUVW XY&Z 1234567890

36 pt CARTOON LIGHT (BAUER)

This was the first script face to reflect the modern comic-strip style of brush lettering, and the first to use only capitals. It was designed by Howard Trafton—designer of the very different formal script that bears his name—and was issued in 1936, with a bold variant.

ABCDEFGHIJ

KLMNOPQR

STUVWXY&Z

abcdefghijklmnop

qrstuvwxyz

£1234567890

ABCDEFGHIJK
LMNOPQRSTU
VWXY&Z

abcdefghijklmn
opqrstuvwxyz

1234567890

48 pt STUDIO BOLD (AMSTERDAM)

This is similar in conception to the previous series, but with the addition of lower-case, although the capitals can be used alone. The light weight was designed by A. Overbeek in 1946, and its bold variant by Dick Dooijes in 1954.

ABCDEFGHIJKLMN OPQRSTUVWXY&Z

CWThQuÆŒ

abcddefghijklmnopqrstu

vwxyz fffiflftndngththtk

æœ 1234567890

48 pt BALZAC (STEMPEL)

This well-formed brush-letter series, designed by Johannes Boehland in 1951, shows
a marked sense of cursive movement and some chancery feeling
in its lower-case alphabet.

65

ABCDEFGHIJKLM
NOPQRSTUVW
XY&Z

abcdefghijklmnopq
rstuvwxyz
1234567890

48 pt ASHLEY SCRIPT 574 (MONOTYPE)

Although issued on Monotype matrices as recently as 1955, this characteristic wet-brush script by Ashley Havinden, was already familiar from its extensive use in his publicity design work since the 1930s. The slightly superior weight of the capitals as compared with the lower-case, and the relatively wide set of the lower-case characters, are representative of the lettering style from which the type series was reproduced.

66

ABCDEFGHIJKLMN
OPQRSTUVW
Æ XYZ Œ

abcdefghijklmnopqrstuvw.

ae xyz œ

1234567890

48 pt MISTRAL (OLIVE/AMSTERDAM)

Designed by Roger Excoffon for Fonderie Olive in 1953, this series has been the most outstandingly successful innovation in the script-type field in recent years. It is strictly a brush letter, but conveys the authentic feel of sophisticated contemporary handwriting un-inhibitedly and unselfconsciously, and has the added virtue of transcending national styles and prejudices.

ABCDEFGHIJKLM NOPQRSTUVW XY&Z

1234567890

abcdefghijklmnopqrstuvw fffi xyz flft

abcdefghijklmnopqrstu fffi vwxyz flft

48 pt ALPHA AND BETA (BAUER)

This complementary pair of series provides alternative lower-case alphabets with capitals common to both. All three are brush formed: the capitals approximate to inclined antique or clarendon, and accompany either a similar sloped-roman lower-case or a simple current script hand showing some chancery influences. Both series were designed by K. F. Bauer and Walter Baum in 1954.

ABCDEFGHI
JKLMNOPQR
STUVW
XY&Z
abcdefghijklmnopqrstu
vwxyz
1234567890

48 pt PALETTE (BERTHOLD)

This brush script, designed by Martin Wilke in 1951, also reflects current chancery
trends in colloquial handwriting, and its unconventionally formed capitals have a
tendency to fall below the alignment of the lower-case.

ABCDEFGHI
JKLMNOPQR
STUVW
XY&Z

abcdefghijklmnopqrstuvwxyz

1234567890

48 pt SLOGAN (NEBIOLO)

A forceful script in relation to its weight, designed by Aldo Novarese in 1957. The
brush treatment extends to rough edges and terminals, and the extension of horizontal
strokes in the capitals beyond their junctions is extremely effective.

ABCDEFGH

IJKLMNOP

QRSTUV

WXYᴣ&Z

abcdefghijklmnopqrst

uvvxyᴣ

1234567890

48 pt PEPITA 613 (MONOTYPE)

This is another brush version of a very individual hand with traces of chancery
influence, in spite of its disarming freedom of angle, alignment and set.
It was designed by Imre Reiner in 1959.

ABCDEFGHIJKLMNOP

QRSTUVWXY&Z

abcdefghijklmnopqrstuvwxyz

1234567890

48 pt CHOC (OLIVE/AMSTERDAM)

This is probably the heaviest of the authentic brush scripts available to date, although it shows no lack of mobility. Its apparent casualness can be misleading: in fact, there is a remarkable consistency of weight and stroke formation throughout both capitals and lower-case and the figures. It was designed by Roger Excoffon for Fonderie Olive in 1955, and has also been available from Amsterdam since 1964.

ABCDEFGHIJKLM NOPQRSTUVW AE XY&Z OE

abcdefghijklmnopqrstuvw
xyzæœ 1234567890 ffifflflftts

54 pt SALTINO (STEMPEL)

The first of these series is a consistently constructed brush script with normally integrated upper and lower-case alphabets. Salto shares the same lower-case as Saltino, but provides oversize capitals with much greater freedom of conception and abrupt shadings. Both series were designed by Karlgeorg Hoefer, and originally issued by the former Klingspor Foundry in 1952 and 1953 respectively.

ABCDEFGH
IJKLMNO
PQRSTUVW
Æ XY&Z Œ
DMNW

abcdefghijklmnopqrstuvwxyz

ff fi fl ft   1234567890   æœ ß rz

54 pt SALTO (STEMPEL)

74

ABCDEFG
HIJKLMN
OPQRSTUV
WXY&Z Th
abcdefghijklmn
opqrstuvwxyz
1234567890

48 pt MAXIM (BAUER)

This powerful, eccentrically drawn brush script designed by Peter Schneidler in
1955 shows many irregularities of inclination and slope in individual letters, but
there is an overall consistency of style and colour
throughout both capitals and lower-case.

75

ABCDEFGHIJ
KLMNOPQRST
UVWXY&Z
abcdefghijklmn
opqrstuvwxyz
œ Æ Œ œ
1234567890

48 pt PAPAGENO (BAUER)

This broad brush treatment of basically simple letter-forms, with rounded outlines
and nearly circular counters, was designed by Richard Weber in 1958.

76

ABCDEFGHIJKL

MNOPQRSTU

UWXY&ZÆŒ

abcdefghijklmnop

qrstuvwxyz

fiflftdgsœœ

1234567890

ABCDEFGHIJ
KLMNOPQR
STUVWXY&Z
abcdefghijklmn
opqrstuvwxyz
fiflftdgs
1234567890

ABCDEFGHIJ
KLMNOPQRSTU
VWXY&ZÆŒ
abcdefghijklmnop
qrstuvwxyz
fiflftdgsœœ
1234567890

48 pt TIME SCRIPT BOLD (WEBER)

This family of three variant weights designed by Professor Georg Trump in 1956 defies classification as regards the nature of the writing instrument employed. All three series are more or less upright, with similar irregularities of height and alignment; some main strokes of the capitals project beyond their junctions; both capitals and lower-case characters exhibit some vestigial serifs; and counters are unenclosed.

ABCDEFGHJKLMNO

PQRSTUVWXY&Z

ÆŒSt Th

abcdefghijklmnopqrstuvw

ff fi fl ft st ss xyz ener ll H th

ch ck 1234567890 æœ

48 pt REPORTER (LUDWIG WAGNER)

Designed by C. Winkow for the former J. Wagner Foundry in 1938, this script series shows many irregularities of alignment and horizontal stroke angles, and an unusual 'texture' that suggests a 'starved brush' treatment.

ABCDEFGHIJK
LMNOPQRSTU
VWXY&Z
abcdefghijklmn
opqrstuvwxyz
1234567890

This basically simple sanserif letter was apparently constructed by means of a succession of partially overlapping pen strokes which combine to produce an irregular halftone effect reminiscent of charcoal drawing technique. Apart from its visibly hand-drawn origin, its classification as a script would be questionable. Stop was designed by Walter Höhnisch in 1939, and both its name and the uncertainty of its status provide an apt conclusion to this representative collection of currently available script types.

List of Script Types, Founders
and Designers

TYPE	FOUNDER	DESIGNER	YEAR
Capitals indicate that the type is shown in this book			
Achtung	Ludwig & Mayer	Erhard Grundeis	1932
Actuelle—see Penflow			
Adagio	Genzsch & Heyse		1939
ADMIRAL SCRIPT	Ludlow	R. Hunter Middleton	1962
Agitator	Typoart	Wolfgang Eickhoff	1960
Aigrette—see Bernhard Tango			
ALPHA (and BETA)	Bauer	K. F. Bauer and Walter Baum	1954
Amanda Ronde	Stephenson Blake	Wagner and Schmidt	1939
AMAZONE	Amsterdam	L. H. D. Smits	1959
Arabella	J. Wagner	A. Drescher	1936
Arabella Favorit	J. Wagner	A. Drescher	1936
Ariadne	Stempel	G. Zapf von Hesse	1954
ARISTON LIGHT	Berthold	Martin Wilke	1933
ARISTON MEDIUM	Berthold	Martin Wilke	1936
Ariston Bold	Berthold	Martin Wilke	1934
Arkona	Genzsch & Heyse	Karl Klaus	1935
Arkona Bold	Genzsch & Heyse	Karl Klaus	1935
Artista	Schelter & Giesecke	Rudolf Steinberg	1936
ARTSCRIPT	Lanston Monotype	Sol Hess	1940
ASHLEY SCRIPT 574	Monotype	Ashley Havinden	1955
Attraktion	Woellmer		1925
Ballerina	Genzsch & Heyse		
Balloon	American Type Founders	M. R. Kaufmann	1939
Balloon Bold	American Type Founders	M. R. Kaufmann	1939
Balloon Extra Bold	American Type Founders	M. R. Kaufmann	1939
BALZAC	Stempel	Johannes Boehland	1951
Bank Script	American Type Founders		1911
Barberina	Woellmer		1925
Bazaar	Stempel	Imre Reiner	1956
Bernhard Brush Script	Bauer	Lucian Bernhard	1928
BERNHARD CURSIVE	Bauer	Lucian Bernhard	1925
BERNHARD CURSIVE BOLD	Bauer	Lucian Bernhard	1928
Bernhard Tango	American Type Founders	Lucian Bernhard	1933

Berolina	Woellmer		1930
Beta—see Alpha			
Bison	Weber	Julius Kim	1955
Bologna	Stephenson Blake		1946
BOULEVARD	Berthold	G. G. Lange	1955
BRAVO	Haas	E. A. Neukomm	1945
Brody	American Type Founders	Harold Broderson	1953
Brush	American Type Founders	Robert E. Smith	1942
Burgund	Schriftguss	Martin Wilke	
Butterfly	Schriftguss	Willy Schumann	1927
Butterfly, Halbfette	Schriftguss	Willy Schumann	1928
Calligraphiques Noires	Deberny & Peignot		1928
CANTATE	Bauer	J. J. Sierck	1958
Caprice	Berthold	Martin Wilke	1939
CARTOON LIGHT	Bauer	H. A. Trafton	1936
Cartoon Bold	Bauer	H. A. Trafton	1936
Champion	Berthold	G. G. Lange	1957
Charme	Ludwig & Mayer	Helmut Matheis	1958
CHOC	Olive	Roger Excoffon	1955
Cigno	Nebiolo	Aldo Novarese	1954
Cigogna	Nebiolo	A. Butti	
CIVILITÉ	American Type Founders	Morris Benton	1922
Clipper	Fonderie Typographique Française		
COMMERCIALSCRIPT	American Typefounders		1925
Copperplate Bold	Stephenson Blake		1953
Coronet	Ludlow	R. Hunter Middleton	1937
Coronet Bold	Ludlow	R. Hunter Middleton	1937
Courier	Typoart	Herbert Thannhaeuser	
DERBY	Berthold	G. G. Lange	1953
DIANE	Olive	Roger Excoffon	1956
DISKUS	Stempel	Martin Wilke	1955
DISKUS SEMI-BOLD	Stempel	Martin Wilke	1955
Divina	Schriftguss	W. Berg	1930
Dom Casual	American Type Founders	Peter Dom	1950
Dom Diagonal	American Type Founders	Peter Dom	1950
Dom Bold	American Type Founders	Peter Dom	1953
DORCHESTER SCRIPT 436	Monotype		
Drescher Eilschrift	Woellmer		1934
Dynamik	Berthold	Herbert Post	1952
Elan	Stempel	Hans Möhring	1937

Energo	Schriftguss	Arnold Drescher	1932
Express	Ludwig & Mayer	Walter Höhnisch	1957
Fanal	Schelter & Giesecke		1933
FLAIR	Ludlow	R. Hunter Middleton	1961
Flamme	Schelter & Giesecke		1933
Flash	Lanston Monotype		
Flash Bold	Lanston Monotype		
Flex	Amsterdam	George Salter	1937
Florentine Cursive	Ludlow	R. Hunter Middleton	1956
Flotte—see Gillies Gothic			
Fluidum	Nebiolo	Aldo Novarese	1951
Fludium Bold	Nebiolo	Aldo Novarese	1951
FORELLE	Weber	Erich Mallowitz	1936
FORELLE AUSZEICHNUNG	Weber	Erich Mallowitz	1936
Forte	Monotype	Carl Reissberger	1962
Fox	Genzsch & Heyse	Walter Rebhuhn	1955
Francesca Ronde	Stephenson Blake		1948
Fresko—see Cartoon			
Gabrielle	Weber	Hans Möhring	1947
Gavotte	Klingspor	Ruds Spemann	1940
GILLIES GOTHIC BOLD	Bauer	W. S. Gillies	1935
GILLIES GOTHIC LIGHT	Bauer	W. S. Gillies	1935
Gladiator	Typoart	Hans Möhring	
Gladiola	Stempel	Martin Wilke	1936
Glenmoy	Stephenson Blake		1932
Gloria	Gans		c 1933
Gong	J. Wagner		1950
Graphic Script—see Lithographica			
GRACIA—see Butterfly			
Graphik	Bauer	Ernst Schneidler	1934
Grayda	American Type Founders	F. H. Riley	1939
Grosvenor Script 493	Monotype		
Hauser Script	Ludlow	George Hauser	1937
Herta—see Butterfly			
Hobby	Genzsch & Heyse	Werner Rebhuhn	1955
Holla	Klingspor	Rudolf Koch	1932
Hoyer Schönschrift	Stempel	Hans T. Hoyer	
IDEAL SCHREIBSCHRIFT 3	Krebs	Franz Riedinger	1927

IMPERIAL SCRIPT	Stephenson Blake		
Imperio	Fundición Tipograficá Nacional		
Impuls	L. Wagner		
Invitation Script	Stephenson Blake		
Jacobea	Berthold	Jacoby-Box	1928
Jiu-Jitsu	Berthold	Hubert Dassel	1936
JULIET	Nebiolo	Aldo Novarese	1955
Junior	Schelter & Giesecke	Hans Heimbeck	1936
Juventud	Gans	Trochut Blanchard	1950
KAUFMANN BOLD	American Type Founders	M. R. Kaufmann	1936
KAUFMANN SCRIPT	American Type Founders	M. R. Kaufmann	1936
Keynote	American Type Founders	W. T. Suiffin	1933
Klaus Kursiv	Genzsch & Heyse	Karl Klaus	1956
Knock-out	Berthold	Hubert Dussel	1936
Kunstlerschreibschrift, Fette	Stempel	Hans Bohn	1957
Lautsprecher	Ludwig & Mayer	J. Erbar	1931
LEGEND	Bauer	Ernst Schneidler	1937
Light Script 351	Monotype		
Liberty	American Type Founders	W. T. Sniffin	1927
Lido	Schriftguss	A. Ausperg	1936
Lithographica	Bauer	Ernst Schneidler	1934
London Script	Stephenson Blake	Imre Reiner	1957
Lotto	Typoart	Herbert Thannhaeuser	1955
LYDIAN CURSIVE	American Type Founders	Warren Chappell	1940
MANDATE	Ludlow	R. Hunter Middleton	1934
MARINA SCRIPT	Stephenson Blake		1936
Matheis-Mobil	Ludwig & Mayer	Helmut Matheis	1960
MAYFAIR CURSIVE	Ludlow	R. Hunter Middleton	1932
Matura	Monotype	Imre Reiner	1938
Miracle	Ludwig & Mayer	Albert Auspurg	1931
MAXIM	Bauer	Peter Schneidler	1955
MERCURIUS	Monotype	Imre Reiner	1957
MISTRAL	Olive	Roger Excoffon	1953
Monoline—see Script Monoline			
Murray Hill	American Type Founders	E. J. Klumpp	1956
Mustang	Stempel		1956
Nova Script	Intertype (USA)	George F. Trenholm	1937
Oleander	Genzsch & Heyse		
Ondine	Deberny & Peignot	A. Frutiger	1954
Orchidea	Schriftguss	K. H. Schaefer	1937
PALACE SCRIPT	Stephenson Blake		1923

PALETTE	Berthold	Martin Wilke	1951
Palomba	Weber	Georg Trump	1955
PAPAGENO	Bauer	Richard Weber	1958
PARISIAN RONDE	Stephenson Blake		1905
Park Avenue	American Type Founders	R. E. Smith	1933
Pentape	Schriftguss	Walter Schnippering	1935
PEPITA	Monotype	Imre Reiner	1959
Petra	Stempel	Heinrich Pariser	1954
Phänomen	Krebs	F. Riedinger	1927
Phyllis—see Wieynck Kursiv			
Polka—see Dom			
Polo	Typoart	Carl Pohl	1960
Prägefest	Ludwig & Mayer	E. Lantenbach	1928
Primadonna	Ludwig & Mayer	Helmut Matheis	1953
Psitt	Fonderie Typographique Française	René Ponot	1953
Pulido	Iranzo		
Radar	Fundición Tipográfica Nacional		
Reiner Black	Berthold	Imre Reiner	1955
REINER SCRIPT	Amsterdam	Imre Reiner	1951
REPORTER	J. Wagner	C. Winkow	1938
Repro Script	American Type Founders	Jerry Mullen	1954
RHAPSODY	Ludwig & Mayer		
Riccardo	Haas		
Romany	American Type Founders	A. R. Bosco	1934
Rondine	Nebiolo	A. Butti	1948
RONDO	Amsterdam	Stefan Schlesinger and Dick Dooijes	1948
RONDO BOLD	Amsterdam		1954
Rusiñol	Fundición Tipográfica Nacional	C. Winkow	
SALTINO	Klingspor	Karlgeorg Hoefer	1953
SALTO	Klingspor	Karlgeorg Hoefer	1952
Saltaretto	Klingspor	Karlgeorg Hoefer	1953
SCRIBE	Deberny & Peignot	Marcel Jacno	1937
Script Monoline 351	Monotype		
SCRIPT BOLD 332—see Prägefest			
Scritto a Lapis	Nebiolo		
Signal Light	Berthold	W. Wege	1932
Signal Medium	Berthold	W. Wege	1931
Signal Bold	Berthold	W. Wege	1932

Sketch	Ludwig & Mayer	Walter Höhnisch	1935
Skizze—see Sketch			
Slogan	Ludwig & Mayer	Helmut Matheis	1959
SLOGAN	Nebiolo	Aldo Novarese	1957
Splendor	Schriftguss	W. Berg	1937
STOP	Ludwig & Mayer	Walter Höhnisch	1939
STRADIVARIUS	Bauer	Imre Reiner	1945
STUDIO	Amsterdam	A. Overbeck	1946
STUDIO BOLD	Amsterdam	Dick Dooijes	1954
Stylo	Fonderie Typographique Française		
Stylescript	Lanston Monotype		
Swing Bold—see Kaufmann Bold			
Temple Script 455	Monotype		
THOMPSON QUILLSCRIPT	American Type Founders	Tommy Thompson	1953
TIME SCRIPT, BOLD	Weber	Georg Trump	1956
TIME SCRIPT, LIGHT	Weber	Georg Trump	1956
TIME SCRIPT, MEDIUM	Weber	Georg Trump	1956
TRAFTON SCRIPT	Bauer	H. A. Trafton	1933
Trinon	Bauer	H. Wieynck	1905
Trocadero Kursiv	Trennert & Sohn	Albert Auspurg	1927
Troubadour Magere	Schriftguss	Willy Schumann	1927
Troubadour Halbfette	Schriftguss	Willy Schumann	1927
Troubadour Lichte	Haas	E. Thiele	1931
UNION PEARL	Stephenson Blake		
Veltro	Nebiolo		1931
Veltro Nero	Nebiolo		1931
Verona	Genzsch & Heyse	Helmut Matheis	1959
Verona (ATF)—see Bologna			
Virtuosa I and II	Stempel	Hermann Zapf	1953
Wave	Ludlow	R. Hunter Middleton	
YOUTHLINE SCRIPT	Stephenson Blake		1952
Wieynck Kursiv	Bauer	H. Wieynck	1911

Bibliography

An Introduction to the History of Printing Types by Geoffrey Dowding (London: Wace; 1961).

A Book of Type & Design by Oldrich Hlavsa (London: Nevill; 1961).

The Encyclopaedia of Type Faces by W. Turner Berry, A. F. Johnson, and W. P. Jaspert (London: Blandford Press; 3rd edition, 1962).

Encyclopaedia Typographica edited by A. J. Bastien (West Drayton, Middlesex: volume I, 1953; volume II, 1961).

Handbook of Early Advertising Art (Typographical Volume) by Clarence P. Hornung (New York: Dover Publications; 3rd edition, 1956).

Alternative Type Faces by Harold E. Waite (London: Technical Publishing Co Ltd; 2nd edition, 1951).

The Western Heritage of Type Design by R. S. Hutchings (London: Cory, Adams & Mackay, 1963).

Index

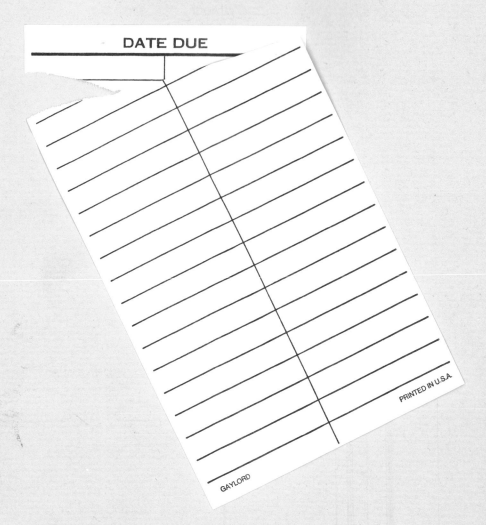

DATE DUE

PRINTED IN U.S.A.

GAYLORD